Spiritual Prosperity Formula Book

Contact Information:

TM3
Property Consulting 2K

contact me @
prosperityconsulting2k@gmail.com

or visit
https://bit.ly/ProsperityConsulting

Table of Contents:

Chapter 1

My Story:

The first time I remember coming in contact with the Bible was in church at a very young age. I would ask my mom questions about the Bible and its stories, and she would explain them to me in a way that I could understand. I remember being fascinated by the stories of Noah's Ark, David and Goliath, Jonah and the whale, and the life of Christ.

As I grew older, I began to read the Bible on my own and found that it provided me with comfort and guidance in my life. In my mid-teens to mid-twenties, the books of Proverbs and Psalms became very impactful to me as I began to see things happen in my life from using the teachings I was learning in these two books.

As my late twenties and early thirties came along, a lot of personal hardships, tragedies, and traumas came with them. The words of Jesus, in particular, resonated with me at this time in my life, and I found myself drawn to his teachings of love, forgiveness, and compassion.

During my darkest moments, I found solace in the Psalms and the book of Job. The raw emotions expressed in these books gave me permission to feel my own pain and grief. I also found comfort in the stories of Joseph, who endured betrayal and imprisonment before rising to a position of power, and Ruth, who remained loyal to her mother-in-law even in the face of great loss. These stories reminded me that even in the midst of hardship, there is hope.

As I continued to study the Bible, I began to see how its teachings could be applied to my everyday life. The commandments to love your neighbor as yourself and to forgive those who have wronged you took on new meaning as I navigated difficult relationships and conflicts. The parables of the Good Samaritan and the Prodigal Son challenged me to examine my own prejudices and to extend grace to those who may not deserve it.

Through it all, the Bible has been a constant source of wisdom, comfort, and inspiration. It has taught me to seek God in all things and to trust in His plan for my life. As I look back on my journey with the Bible, I am grateful for the ways in which it has shaped me and helped me become the person I am today. The Bible has become the cornerstone of my faith and has helped me navigate the ups and downs of life.

Going forward in this book, I will show you the tools God showed me that allowed me to get in alignment with him and his laws in the spiritual and physical realm. When you get in alignment with him, you'll find there is nothing you cannot do with him right there by your side for this ride we call life. Most importantly, I hope my story and this book help those who are at their lowest point in life and just cannot see a way out. Just know there is no problem too big for our God. God bless you, and let this book help you for years to come.

Knowledge:

Chapter 2

The Bible - Your 1st Prosperity Tool

Part 1: Knowledge

Instruction Manual for Living a Prosperous Life:

The Bible is a timeless book that has been around for centuries, offering guidance and wisdom to those seeking to live a prosperous life. It is considered an instruction manual full of stories and lessons that can be applied to daily life. Through its teachings, the Bible provides valuable insight into how to handle difficult situations, be a good citizen, and live a life of faith and integrity. It is an invaluable resource for those seeking personal growth and improvement in all aspects of life.

The Bible is a powerful tool for personal growth and spiritual development, helping individuals understand God's will and plan for their lives. It encourages a life of faith, love, and obedience to God and provides comfort and strength during difficult times. It serves as a guide for a prosperous life, offering timeless wisdom, guidance, and insight to anyone seeking a better way of living aligned with God's will.

Energy, Frequency, and Vibration in the Bible:

The Bible is rich in spiritual knowledge and wisdom, and it often speaks of energy, frequency, and vibration. These concepts are woven throughout scripture and play a significant role in understanding the power of God.

In the book of Genesis, God creates the universe through the power of His spoken words, demonstrating the concept of vibration. The book of Psalms speaks of the power of God's word as a hammer, emphasizing the impact of frequency. Proverbs compare God's word to fire, illuminating the idea of energy. These examples highlight the importance of energy, frequency, and vibration in the Bible and how they contribute to understanding the power of God.

Prayer is also emphasized as a form of energy, frequency, and vibration that can bring about positive change in our lives. When we pray, we send out a powerful wave of energy that can be used for healing, protection, and miracles. The Bible highlights the significance of prayer and its potential to bring about positive change.

In conclusion, the Bible is a source of spiritual knowledge and wisdom that delves deeply into the concepts of energy, frequency, and vibration. These ideas play a crucial role in understanding the power of God and can be applied to our daily lives. Through its teachings, the Bible encourages us to harness the power of energy, frequency, and vibration to achieve a prosperous life aligned with God's will.

Part 2: Action

How to Use the Bible as Your 1st Prosperity Tool:

The Bible is not just a religious book; it contains valuable wisdom and insights that can be applied to everyday life. Its teachings can serve as a source of guidance and inspiration for anyone seeking personal growth and development, regardless of their religious background.

Proverbs and Psalms are two books in the Bible that offer timeless and relevant wisdom. Proverbs is a book of wise sayings that offers practical advice on various topics, such as how to live a good life and how to handle relationships. Psalms is a collection of songs and prayers that provide comfort and peace in difficult times.

To fully benefit from the Bible's teachings, approach it with an open mind and heart, seeing it as a comprehensive guidebook that can provide valuable guidance and inspiration. Leave any preconceived notions at the door and be open to new ideas and perspectives.

Regular study of the Bible is key to unlocking its full potential. Set aside time each day or week to read and study its teachings. The

Bible can be a challenging text to navigate, so have resources and tools to help understand its message fully. Joining a Bible study group, attending church, or using study aids like concordances, commentaries, or devotionals can help in the journey.

The Bible's teachings are meant to be meditated on and internalized. Take time to reflect on the lessons and teachings and consider how they apply to life. Journaling, prayer, or mindfulness exercises can be useful in helping connect more deeply with the teachings of the Bible.

The wisdom and insights of the Bible are valuable only if they are applied to life. Consider how the teachings of the Bible can be applied to daily routines, relationships, and decision-making processes. Living a life aligned with the teachings of the Bible can help achieve the prosperity and abundance desired.

Ultimately, the Bible reminds us that God has a plan for our lives, and it's up to us to trust in that plan. Even when things may not go as expected or hoped, the Bible encourages trust in God's plan and seeks His guidance in all aspects of life.

In conclusion, the Bible can be a powerful tool in transforming life and achieving prosperity. By approaching it with an open mind and heart, regularly studying its teachings, meditating on its messages, applying its insights to life, and seeking God's guidance, the full benefits of this valuable resource can be experienced. Begin exploring the Bible today and discover how it can assist in reaching aspirations and living a prosperous life.

All Scripture is breathed out by God and profitable for teaching, rebuking, correcting, and training in righteousness - 2 Timothy 3:16

Chapter 3

Book of Proverbs - Knowledge & Wisdom Scriptures

Part 1: Knowledge

What is the Book of Proverbs

The Book of Proverbs is a book from the Hebrew Bible, also known as the Tanakh or the Old Testament. This collection of wise sayings and instructions was written by King Solomon and other wise men of Israel, and it provides guidance and advice for living a successful and godly life. With 31 chapters filled with wisdom and practical advice on how to live a good and moral life, the Book of Proverbs is still relevant today.

King Solomon, the son of King David, is said to have written 3,000 proverbs, which were later collected and compiled into the Book of Proverbs. The book is divided into 31 chapters, each containing a collection of these wise sayings and instructions. Proverbs are written in a poetic form and often use metaphors and similes to illustrate their teachings and make them more memorable.

The purpose of the proverbs in the Book of Proverbs is to provide guidance and instruction for living a life of wisdom and righteousness. The teachings encourage people to make wise decisions and to live with integrity. They remind us to be humble and to seek God's guidance in all our decisions. The book is also a source of inspiration and comfort, reminding us of God's presence and His role as a source of wisdom and guidance.

The Book of Proverbs is not only a historical document, but also a timeless guide for personal and spiritual growth. It provides comfort and inspiration for those who seek to live a life of wisdom and righteousness. The book's concise, memorable sayings offer guidance on everything from ethical behavior to practical living, making it a valuable resource for those looking to grow in their faith and lead a virtuous life.

The Power of Proverbs

The book of Proverbs is a collection of ancient wisdom that has been passed down through generations. It contains wise sayings and practical advice that can be applied to everyday life. The book is a great source of guidance for anyone seeking insight into their lives and how to live a meaningful and fulfilling life.

The book of Proverbs teaches valuable lessons, such as humility, wisdom, patience, faith in God, and the importance of thinking before acting, being kind and generous, and being honest and trustworthy. By following the advice in the book, one can become a better person and lead a more fulfilling life.

The book of Proverbs is an invaluable source of wisdom that helps in navigating the complexities of life. It offers timeless insights and guidance on how to live a virtuous and successful life. The proverbs cover a wide range of topics, including building strong relationships, achieving financial prosperity, and more.

Reading and studying the book of Proverbs can help one gain a deeper understanding of themselves, the world around them, and their relationship with God. It is not just a historical text but a guide for living a purposeful, integral, and wise life in the present.

Part 2: Action

How to Use Your 2nd Prosperity Tool: Proverbs

Are you feeling lost or uncertain about how to achieve your goals or overcome life's challenges? The book of Proverbs in the Bible offers practical advice and timeless wisdom that can guide you towards success and fulfillment.

Proverbs emphasizes the importance of wisdom, understanding, and making wise choices based on a deep understanding of the world around you. By reading and reflecting on its words, you can gain insight into how to approach your goals with wisdom and focus.

One of the most critical themes in Proverbs is the importance of staying committed to your goals. Proverbs 16:3 advises us to "Commit your works to the Lord, and your thoughts will be established." In other words, committing your goals and plans to God can help you stay focused and motivated to achieve them.

Another key theme in Proverbs is the power of a positive attitude. Proverbs 17:22 says, "A merry heart does good, like medicine, but a broken spirit dries the bones." Cultivating a positive outlook can have a powerful impact on your well-being and help you overcome obstacles on your path to success.

Trusting in God's plan for your life is also a crucial message in Proverbs. Proverbs 3:5-6 advises us to "Trust in the Lord with all your heart and lean not on your own understanding. In all your ways acknowledge Him, and He will make your paths straight." By trusting in God and seeking His guidance, you can stay on the path towards your goals and fulfill your purpose.

In summary, Proverbs is a valuable resource for personal growth and development. By applying its wisdom to your life, you can make wise choices, stay committed to your goals, maintain a positive attitude, and trust in God's plan for your life. Take the time to explore the power of Proverbs today and unlock its potential for a prosperous and fulfilling life.

Wisdom is the principal thing; Therefore get wisdom. And in all your getting, get understanding. - Proverbs 4:7

Chapter 4

Book of Psalms - Spiritual Warfare Scriptures

Part 1: Knowledge

What is the Book of Psalms

The Book of Psalms is a collection of 150 poetic songs, prayers, and hymns written by various authors over centuries. King David is believed to have written the majority of the Psalms, which are divided into five books.

This sacred book offers a rich tapestry of human emotions, covering various themes such as praise for God, lamentation for sin, and expressions of faith in God's goodness and power. It provides guidance for living a life of faith and service to God, inspiring and comforting readers throughout history.

Psalms are widely read and translated into many languages. Its timeless messages of faith, hope, and love continue to provide comfort and hope to people worldwide, regardless of their beliefs. Its poetic and musical nature makes it a beautiful source of encouragement and peace.

The Book of Psalms is used in Jewish, Christian, and Muslim worship and has been set to music in various forms. The themes of praise, thanksgiving, trust in God, and petition for help in times of trouble are prevalent throughout the book, making it a treasured collection of prayers and hymns. The Book of Psalms is not just a historical text but a source of comfort and guidance for anyone seeking to live a life of faith and devotion.

Psalms vs Spiritual Warfare

The Book of Psalms is a collection of ancient Hebrew poems and prayers that express a wide range of emotions and serve as a means of communication with God. It provides comfort, guidance, and inspiration to those seeking to live a life of faith and devotion.

On the other hand, spiritual warfare refers to the ongoing conflict between good and evil, God and the devil, for the souls of people and the world. It is a core belief for many Christians and is fought on a spiritual level. The Bible, including the Book of Psalms, is seen as a powerful weapon in this spiritual warfare, offering guidance, encouragement, and protection.

The Psalms have a special role in spiritual warfare as they can be used for praising God, asking for protection, seeking guidance, rebuking the enemy, and declaring victory over spiritual battles. They serve as a powerful reminder of God's love and power and can strengthen individuals in their spiritual battles.

In conclusion, while the concepts of Psalms and spiritual warfare are distinct, they are closely related as the Psalms can be used as a tool in the practice of spiritual warfare. By incorporating the teachings and prayers of the Book of Psalms into their spiritual lives, individuals can find guidance and strength in their battles against evil and draw closer to God.

Part 2: Action

How to use your 3rd Prosperity Tool: Psalms

Life is full of challenges and struggles, and it's easy to feel overwhelmed and discouraged. Whether you're facing personal obstacles or striving to achieve your goals, it can be difficult to stay motivated and focused. But there is a source of comfort and motivation that has helped people for centuries: the book of Psalms.

The Psalms are a collection of poems and prayers that can provide us with a sense of hope and strength as we navigate life's challenges. By reading and reflecting on the words of Psalms, we can gain insight into our own lives and find the courage to face our struggles.

To use Psalms as a tool for prosperity, we can start by incorporating them into our daily routine. We can set aside time each day to read and reflect on a Psalm that resonates with us or speaks to our current situation. This can be done as part of our morning or evening routine, or during a quiet moment in the day.

When reading a Psalm, we can focus on the key themes and messages, such as the power of prayer, perseverance, faith, and community. We can use these themes as a guide for our own lives, and apply them to our personal goals and challenges.

For example, if we are struggling to stay motivated to achieve a goal, we can read Psalms 126:5 and remind ourselves that even when we face difficult times, we can still achieve our goals if we remain committed and keep pushing forward.

If we are feeling overwhelmed and discouraged, we can read Psalms 31:24 and remind ourselves to have faith in God and ourselves, and to be of good courage.

We can also use the Psalms as a tool for reflection and gratitude. By reflecting on the blessings in our lives and expressing gratitude for them, we can cultivate a more positive outlook and attract more prosperity into our lives.

In conclusion, the Psalms are a valuable tool for prosperity and can provide us with the strength, courage, and motivation to achieve our goals and navigate life's challenges. By incorporating them into our daily routine and focusing on their key themes and messages, we can use the Psalms to guide us towards a more fulfilling and prosperous life.

For God alone, my soul waits in silence, for my hope is from Him. He alone is my rock and my salvation, my fortress; I shall not be shaken. - Psalm 62:5-6

Chapter 5

God's 11 Forgotten Laws - Life laws you should master

Part 1: Knowledge

Law of Thinking

The Law of Thinking is a concept that has been studied and practiced by those seeking personal development and success. It suggests that our thoughts have a powerful impact on our lives and the world around us. This concept has been present in religious texts for centuries, including the Bible.

The Bible offers valuable insight into the power of our thoughts and the impact they can have on our lives. Proverbs 23:7 states, "As a man thinketh in his heart, so is he." This verse suggests that our thoughts shape our reality and that our innermost beliefs and desires can have a significant impact on our lives.

In Matthew 21:22, Jesus says, "And whatever things you ask in prayer, believing, you will receive." This verse highlights the importance of having faith in our thoughts and beliefs. When we truly believe in something and have faith that it will come to fruition, we are more likely to receive it in our lives.

The Bible also emphasizes the importance of positive thinking and focusing on what is good. Philippians 4:8 states, "Finally, brethren, whatever things are true, whatever things are noble, whatever things are just, whatever things are pure, whatever things are lovely, whatever things are of good report, if there is any virtue and if there is anything praiseworthy—meditate on these things." This verse encourages us to focus on positive thoughts and to avoid negative thinking and dwelling on things that are not beneficial to our well-being.

The Law of Thinking and the Bible also emphasize the power of visualization. In Habakkuk 2:2, the prophet Habakkuk is instructed to "write the vision and make it plain on tablets, that he may run whoever reads it." This verse suggests that visualizing our goals and desires can help bring them to fruition. When we can see what we want and believe that it is possible, we are more likely to achieve it.

In summary, the Law of Thinking and the Bible both emphasize the importance of our thoughts and beliefs in shaping our lives. By focusing on positive thinking, having faith in our beliefs, and visualizing our goals, we can create a reality that is aligned with our desires and aspirations. The Bible can serve as a valuable resource for wisdom and guidance in our journey towards personal development and success.

Law of Supply

The Bible emphasizes the Law of Supply and the importance of having faith in God's provision. The concept of abundance is central to many of the Bible's teachings, such as the story of the loaves and fishes, where Jesus multiplied the food to feed the multitudes. This demonstrates the principle of abundance and the limitless potential of God's provision.

The Bible teaches that we should not worry about our needs because God knows what we need before we even ask. By seeking first the kingdom of God and His righteousness, we can receive all the things we need, as God will provide for us.

Gratitude is also a crucial aspect of the Law of Supply in the Bible. We are instructed to give thanks in all circumstances and to be content with what we have, knowing that God will provide for us. This attitude of gratitude and contentment opens the door to more blessings and abundance.

The Bible emphasizes asking and taking action as key components of the Law of Supply. We are encouraged to ask God for what we need and to have faith that it will be provided. At the same time, we are also called to take action toward our goals and not just wait for things to happen.

In conclusion, the Law of Supply is a fundamental principle that can be found in both the Bible and the teachings of personal growth. By focusing on abundance, gratitude, taking action, and having faith in God's provision, we can unlock the universal flow of abundance and create a life filled with prosperity and fulfillment.

Law of Attraction

The Law of Attraction is a concept that has been around for centuries and is deeply rooted in the teachings of the Bible. The Bible highlights the power of faith, belief, and positive thinking in attracting blessings and prosperity into our lives. Positive thinking and faith are evident throughout scripture, and they are key components in attracting the life we desire.

The Bible teaches us that faith is the key to unlocking the power of the Law of Attraction. It states that whatever we ask for in prayer, we will receive if we believe that we will receive it. This reinforces the idea that our thoughts and beliefs shape our reality and that positive energy attracts positive experiences. By having faith and focusing on positive thoughts, we can create the life we desire and attract blessings and abundance into our lives.

Moreover, the Bible emphasizes the power of gratitude, as it is mentioned repeatedly throughout scripture. Gratitude is essential in attracting positive experiences and living a fulfilling life. By expressing gratitude for what we have, we open ourselves up to receiving even more blessings and abundance. Positive energy attracts more positive energy, and being grateful is a powerful way to attract more blessings into our lives.

The Bible also teaches us the power of visualization, as it is mentioned throughout scripture. Visualization is a powerful tool in receiving our desires, as it allows us to imagine ourselves living the life we desire. By visualizing our desires and focusing on the positive feelings associated with them, we can attract those experiences into our lives. This aligns with the Law of Attraction, as the power of positive thoughts and feelings attracts positive experiences.

In summary, the Law of Attraction is a universal principle deeply rooted in the teachings of the Bible. By having faith, expressing gratitude, and visualizing our desires, we can attract the life we desire and blessings and abundance into our lives. The power of positive thinking and faith is evident throughout scripture, and it is a key component in achieving prosperity and living a fulfilling life. By aligning our thoughts, feelings, and actions with the teachings of the Bible, we can unlock the power of the Law of Attraction and create a more joyful and abundant life.

Law of Receiving

The Bible contains valuable teachings on the power of receiving and giving. In Luke 6:38, it states, "Give, and it will be given to you. A good measure, pressed down, shaken together, and running over, will be poured into your lap. For with the measure you use, it will be measured to you." This verse emphasizes the importance of giving and how it can lead to abundance and joy in our lives.

The Bible also teaches us to be open and receptive to blessings and opportunities. In Matthew 7:7-8, it says, "Ask, and it will be given to you; seek, and you will find; knock, and the door will be opened to you. For everyone who asks receives; the one who seeks finds; and to the one who knocks, the door will be opened." This verse encourages us to be proactive in seeking blessings and to have faith that we will receive them.

Additionally, the Bible teaches us to have faith and trust in the divine plan for our lives. Jeremiah 29:11 says, "For I know the plans I have for you," declares the Lord, "plans to prosper you and not to harm you, plans to give you hope and a future." This verse reminds us that there is a plan for our lives, and by having faith and trust in it, we can receive the abundance and joy that we desire.

In conclusion, the Law of Receiving is a powerful principle that can help us achieve the life we desire. By being open and willing to receive blessings and opportunities, consistently giving to those in need, and aligning our actions with our desires, we can attract abundance and joy into our lives. The Bible provides valuable teachings on the power of giving, receiving, and faith, which can help us unlock the full potential of this law in our lives.

Law of Increase

The Law of Increase is a powerful principle that is deeply rooted in the teachings of the Bible. By focusing on gratitude, appreciation, and praise, we can attract more positive energy and experiences into our lives. The Bible provides valuable teachings on the power of gratitude and faith, which can help us unlock the full potential of this law in our lives.

The Law of Increase also emphasizes the importance of generosity and giving. In 2 Corinthians 9:6-8, it says, "Whoever sows sparingly will also reap sparingly, and whoever sows bountifully will also reap bountifully. Each one must give as he has decided in his heart, not reluctantly or under compulsion, for God loves a cheerful giver. And God is able to make all grace abound to you, so that having all sufficiency in all things at all times, you may abound in every good work." This passage emphasizes the importance of giving generously and cheerfully, as it leads to abundance and joy.

The Law of Increase also reminds us that we have the power to control our thoughts and beliefs. In Philippians 4:8, it says, "Finally, brothers, whatever is true, whatever is honorable, whatever is just, whatever is pure, whatever is lovely, whatever is commendable, if there is any excellence, if there is anything worthy of praise, think about these things." This verse encourages us to focus our thoughts and beliefs on positive things, which can attract more positivity and abundance into our lives.

In conclusion, the Law of Increase is a powerful principle that can help us achieve the life we desire. By embracing generosity and giving, expressing gratitude and praise, trusting in God's provision, and focusing on positive thoughts and beliefs, we can attract more abundance and joy into our lives. The Bible provides valuable teachings on the power of gratitude, faith, and generosity, which can help us unlock the full potential of this law in our lives.

Law of Compensation

The Law of Compensation is a universal principle that has been explored in various spiritual and personal growth teachings. The Bible, in particular, contains valuable insights into this law and how it relates to our lives. One of the most well-known examples is the Parable of the Talents, which emphasizes the importance of taking action toward our desires and using the resources we have been given to achieve abundance.

Another important lesson from the Bible is the concept of sowing and reaping. This principle emphasizes the importance of taking responsibility for our actions and choices, and how they can lead to either positive or negative consequences. By sowing positive actions and choices, we can attract positive outcomes and blessings into our lives.

Furthermore, the Bible emphasizes the importance of generosity and giving to others. This principle aligns with the Law of Compensation, as giving to others can lead to abundance in our own lives. By being generous with our resources and helping others, we can create a positive flow of energy that attracts more positivity and abundance into our lives.

Overall, the Law of Compensation is a powerful force in our lives that can lead to abundance and fulfillment. By being conscious of our thoughts, beliefs, and actions, and by following the principles of planning, acquiring tools, and taking action, we can tap into this power and achieve our desires. The Bible provides valuable teachings on the Law of Compensation, including the importance of taking action, sowing and reaping, and being generous. By applying these teachings to our lives, we can live a life of abundance and fulfillment.

Law of Non-Resistance

The Law of Non-Resistance is a concept that is deeply rooted in the teachings of the Bible. In Matthew 5:39, Jesus says, "But I tell you, do not resist an evil person. If anyone slaps you on the right cheek, turn to them the other cheek also." This passage encourages us to let go of resistance and not retaliate when we are wronged. Instead, we are called to respond with love and forgiveness, which can create a more harmonious and peaceful world.

The Bible also teaches us to trust in God's plan and not to resist the changes and challenges that come our way. In Proverbs 3:5-6, we are reminded to "Trust in the Lord with all your heart and lean not on your understanding; in all your ways submit to him, and he will make your paths straight." By trusting in God's plan and accepting what comes our way, we can find peace and joy even in difficult circumstances.

By embracing the Law of Non-Resistance and cultivating a positive, loving mindset, we can attract positivity into our lives and live a more fulfilling life. The Bible provides valuable teachings on the importance of letting go of resistance and accepting the challenges and changes that come our way. By applying these teachings to our lives, we can live a life of greater peace, harmony, and fulfillment.

Law of Forgiveness

The importance of forgiveness is a prominent theme in the Bible. Jesus often spoke about forgiveness and its necessity, emphasizing the need for his followers to forgive others as they themselves seek forgiveness. The reciprocal nature of forgiveness is highlighted in the Lord's Prayer, where we ask for forgiveness for our own sins as we forgive those who have wronged us.

Forgiveness is not just a suggestion but a commandment in the Bible. Matthew 6:14-15 states that "if you forgive others their trespasses, your heavenly Father will also forgive you. But if you do not forgive others their trespasses, neither will your Father forgive your trespasses." This passage highlights the importance of forgiveness in our relationship with God.

Love is also closely linked to the concept of forgiveness in the Bible. 1 Corinthians 13:4-7 describes love as patient, kind, humble, and unselfish. It does not seek its way, does not get angry, and rejoices in the truth. Forgiveness is an act of love, as it involves bearing with others, believing in their ability to change, and enduring difficult situations.

In conclusion, the Law of Forgiveness and the teachings of the Bible both stress the importance of letting go of past hurt and resentment, cultivating empathy and compassion towards others, and creating a more harmonious and peaceful existence. By embracing forgiveness, we can achieve personal growth, cultivate deeper relationships, and lead a more fulfilling and meaningful life.

Law of Sacrifice

The Law of Sacrifice is a principle deeply rooted in the teachings of the Bible. Sacrifice was an important part of religious rituals in the Bible, and sacrifices were made to atone for sins and show devotion to God. The New Testament teaches that Jesus Christ is the ultimate sacrifice for humanity's sins.

Beyond literal sacrifices, the Bible also teaches the importance of sacrificing personal desires and putting others first. Selflessness is seen as a crucial aspect of living a Christian life, and Jesus modeled this behavior through his teachings and actions. Christians are called to put aside personal desires and "die to self" for the benefit of others.

The Bible also stresses the value of discipline and self-control, emphasizing the importance of resisting temptation and living a life of moral and spiritual integrity. This requires individuals to sacrifice immediate gratification for long-term success and fulfillment.

Ultimately, the Law of Sacrifice and its biblical counterparts teach us that success and fulfillment require effort, commitment, and sacrifice. By sacrificing personal desires, practicing discipline, and prioritizing the well-being of others, individuals can achieve their goals and live a more meaningful and fulfilling life.

Law of Obedience

In the Bible, obedience is a fundamental principle of faith that is emphasized throughout scripture. It is viewed as a way to demonstrate love and devotion to God and as a means of receiving blessings and protection. The Bible highlights the importance of following God's commandments and living a life that is aligned with His will, and obedience is seen as key to living a fulfilling and blessed life.

The Book of Proverbs states that "The fear of the Lord is the beginning of wisdom, and knowledge of the Holy One is understanding" (Proverbs 9:10). This suggests that obedience to God's commandments is the foundation of true wisdom and understanding and is essential for living a successful and meaningful life.

Moreover, the Bible emphasizes the importance of obedience in relationships with others, such as children obeying their parents and employees obeying their employers. In the book of Colossians, it is written, "Children, obey your parents in everything, for this pleases the Lord" (Colossians 3:20), highlighting the significance of obedience in familial relationships.

Ultimately, the Law of Obedience and its biblical counterparts remind us of the importance of submitting to God's will and embracing obedience in all areas of our lives. By following God's commandments and respecting those in positions of authority, we can experience the blessings and protection that come with a life of obedience.

Law of Success

The Bible provides guidance on the path to success. Proverbs 16:3 states, "Commit to the Lord whatever you do, and he will establish your plans." This emphasizes the importance of aligning one's actions with God's will and trusting in His plan for our lives. Proverbs 3:5-6 reminds us to trust in the Lord and not lean on our understanding, acknowledging that God will guide us in the right direction.

Humility is also a key aspect of success according to the Bible. Proverbs 11:2 states, "When pride comes, then comes disgrace, but with humility comes wisdom." This verse emphasizes the importance of being humble and recognizing that success is not solely the result of our efforts but rather a combination of our hard work and the blessings and guidance of God.

Time is a valuable resource, and it is important to use it constructively towards one's success. The power of positive affirmations should not be underestimated. By repeating affirmations such as "I CAN" and truly believing in them, individuals can unlock their full potential and move towards their goals with confidence.

Overall, the Law of Success and the teachings of the Bible provide valuable insights into the principles necessary for achieving one's goals and living a fulfilling life. By embracing these principles and cultivating the mindset and habits necessary for success, individuals can live a life that aligns with their purpose and goals.

Part 2: Action

Working with God: Your 4th Prosperity Tool

The universe operates according to natural laws that govern the way things work. Understanding and working with these laws can help us achieve our goals and live a fulfilling life. In this chapter, we will explore the three most important laws that can help us tap into the power of the universe and receive our desires: the Law of Attraction, the Law of Vibration, and the Law of Cause and Effect.

The Law of Attraction states that we attract into our lives what we focus on. Our thoughts and emotions have a powerful effect on our reality, so it's crucial to cultivate positivity and optimism to achieve our goals. By focusing on our desired outcomes, visualizing success, and maintaining a positive mindset, we can attract the people and circumstances that will help us achieve our dreams.

The Law of Vibration teaches us that everything in the universe vibrates at a specific frequency. We can use this knowledge to align ourselves with the energy of our desires. By raising our vibration through positive thoughts and emotions, we can attract the people and circumstances that match our desires.

The Law of Cause and Effect is also known as the Law of Action. It teaches us that our actions and energy have an equal and opposite reaction from the things we do. To bring our desires into reality, we must take inspired action toward our goals. This can include setting intentions, taking small steps towards our goals every day, and practicing gratitude for what we already have.

To work with these laws effectively, we must cultivate a sense of faith and trust in the universe's plan for us. When we align ourselves with the natural laws of the universe, God will bless us with abundance and joy in our lives. By focusing on the steps outlined in this chapter and committing to working with the laws, we can achieve our goals and receive our desires.

In conclusion, working with the laws of the universe can be a powerful tool for achieving our goals and living a fulfilling life. By understanding and working with the Law of Attraction, the Law of Vibration, and the Law of Cause and Effect, we can tap into the power of the universe and receive our desires. By aligning ourselves with the natural laws of the universe, we can open ourselves up to abundance and joy in our lives. Let's take the first step towards a more fulfilling and prosperous life by applying these principles in our daily lives.

Jesus replied, "Anyone who loves me will obey my teaching. My Father will love them, and we will come to them and make our home with them." - John 14:23

Action:

Chapter 6

Mind Reels - You create the movies and pictures that go into your mind

Part 1: Knowledge

Having a clear vision of what you want to achieve is an essential part of setting and achieving goals. It is important to effectively manage the images and ideas in your mind to stay focused on your goals. When you have a clear and vivid picture of what you want to accomplish, it can help you stay motivated and inspired to keep working towards your goal.

The mental images in your mind are like a roadmap to success, guiding you towards your desired outcome. They help you stay on course and remind you of why you are working towards a particular goal. By visualizing the result of your efforts, and imagining yourself achieving it, you can remain motivated and excited about the process of reaching your goal.

Moreover, managing the mental pictures in your mind can also help you stay on track and avoid getting sidetracked. A clear and vivid image of what you want to achieve can help you stay focused on the necessary steps needed to reach your goal, and avoid getting distracted by other things.

In summary, managing the mental images and ideas in your mind is a crucial component of setting and achieving goals. It can help you remain motivated, focused, disciplined, and on track towards success. Having a clear vision of what you want to achieve is an essential element of achieving your goals, and effectively managing the images and ideas in your mind can help you get there.

Part 2: Action

How to use your 5th Prosperity Tool

Visualization is a potent and transformative tool that can aid in achieving our goals by creating a mental image of our desired outcome. It taps into the power of the mind and the universe, allowing us to manifest our desires through the power of intention.

To effectively use visualization, it's important to have a clear mental image of what we want to achieve, accompanied by positive emotions and beliefs. This can help us stay motivated, focused, and confident, which can aid in overcoming challenges and obstacles.

Visualization can also help reprogram our subconscious mind, replacing negative thoughts and beliefs with positive ones. This shift can create a more empowering and supportive mindset, which can facilitate the achievement of our goals.

In addition to visualization, it's important to take inspired action towards our goals. Visualization can help us stay focused and motivated, but action is necessary to bring our desires into reality.

In conclusion, visualization is a powerful tool that can help us achieve our goals by creating a clear mental image of our desired outcome. When combined with positive emotions, beliefs, and inspired action, visualization can be a transformative force in our lives. So, take the time to visualize your desired outcomes, stay focused on your goals, and take inspired action towards achieving them. The power of visualization is within your reach.

"Ask and it will be given to you; seek and you will find; knock and the door will be opened to you. - Matthew 7:7

Chapter 7

Gratitude List - Give the Lord praise for the things you have and don't have at the moment

Part 1: Knowledge

Gratitude is a powerful emotion that can transform our lives, and creating a gratitude list is an effective way to cultivate and enhance this feeling. The first step in creating a gratitude list is to take a moment to reflect on what you are truly grateful for. This can be anything from the simple pleasures of life, such as a beautiful sunset, to more significant blessings, such as a supportive family or good health.

Once you have identified what you are grateful for, it's important to take the time to reflect on why you are grateful for each item on your list. This can help to deepen your appreciation and create a stronger connection to what you are thankful for. For example, if you are grateful for your job, reflect on how your work makes a positive impact on your life and the lives of others.

Practicing mindfulness is also crucial when creating a gratitude list. This involves being fully present in the moment and appreciating the things that you are grateful for right now. For instance, if you are thankful for a supportive friend, take the time to think about how this person is currently impacting your life and express your gratitude to them.

Finally, to make gratitude a habit, set aside a specific time each day to reflect on what you are grateful for, and write down your thoughts in a journal or on a piece of paper. Throughout the day, try to maintain a positive outlook and focus on the things that you are thankful for. Over time, this practice can become a powerful tool for staying motivated, focused, and positive, and can help you build a fulfilling and meaningful life.

Part 2: Action

How to use your 6th Prosperity Tool

Gratitude is a transformative force that can help us achieve our goals and live a more fulfilling life. By shifting our focus to the positive things in our lives and cultivating an attitude of appreciation and contentment, we can tap into the power of gratitude to achieve our dreams.

Making a daily gratitude list is a simple yet effective way to stay motivated and focused on our goals. By taking the time to recognize and appreciate the good things in our lives, we can shift our mindset to be more optimistic and motivated. This can help us stay on track and put in the necessary hard work to achieve our goals.

Moreover, gratitude has a positive impact on our overall well-being, reducing stress and anxiety and increasing our sense of happiness and fulfillment. By focusing on the positive, we can reduce negative thoughts and emotions that can hold us back from achieving our goals.

Creating a gratitude list is easy. Simply take a few minutes each day to write down the things you are grateful for, big or small. It can include people, experiences, opportunities, or even small moments of joy. The key is to focus on the positive and cultivate an attitude of appreciation for the good things in your life.

Making gratitude a daily habit can also help reprogram our subconscious mind, which can affect our behavior and actions. By focusing on the positive, we can create a more empowering and supportive mindset that helps us achieve our goals and live a more fulfilling life.

In conclusion, gratitude is a powerful tool that can help us achieve our goals and live a happier, more fulfilling life. By creating a daily gratitude list and cultivating an attitude of appreciation and contentment, we can tap into the power of gratitude to achieve our dreams. So, take the time each day to make a gratitude list, and watch as your mindset and perspective shift to one that is more optimistic, empowered, and focused on achieving your goals.

I will give thanks to you, Lord, with all my heart; I will tell of all your wonderful deeds. - Psalm 9:1

Chapter 8

Prayer - Personal time w/ God!!

Part 1: Knowledge

Prayer is powerful and has the potential to help individuals in all aspects of their lives, including achieving their goals. Throughout the Bible, numerous stories and verses emphasize the importance of prayer and trusting God's plan. By incorporating biblical prayer into our daily lives, we can gain insight and strength to help us reach our goals.

The Bible is a rich source of encouragement for prayer. Philippians 4:6-7 states, "Do not be anxious about anything, but in every situation, by prayer and petition, with thanksgiving, present your requests to God. And the peace of God, which transcends all understanding, will guard your hearts and your minds in Christ Jesus." This verse reminds us that we can come to God with our requests and that He will provide peace and understanding.

Prayer can also be a source of strength for those working towards their goals. Isaiah 40:31 says, "But those who hope in the Lord will renew their strength. They will soar on wings like eagles; they will run and not grow weary, they will walk and not faint." This verse reminds us that when we put our hope in God, He will give us the strength to persevere and overcome obstacles in our journey towards our goals.

By utilizing biblical prayer, individuals can gain insight and strength to help them achieve their goals. Whether it be for guidance, comfort, or strength, prayer can be a valuable tool in helping individuals focus on what is important and provide peace and clarity during difficult times. By incorporating prayer into their lives, individuals can find the courage to take risks and make changes necessary to reach their goals. So, take the time each day to pray and trust in God's plan for your life, and watch as He guides you towards achieving your goals.

Part 2: Action

How to use your 7th Prosperity Tool

Prayer is a tool that can help us accomplish our goals by connecting us with God and allowing us to seek His guidance and help. The Bible teaches us that prayer is a way to communicate with God and to seek His will for our lives.

Through prayer, we can ask God for the strength and courage to persevere through difficult times and to stay focused on our goals. By seeking His help, we can tap into His infinite wisdom and gain insight and clarity about the steps we need to take to achieve our goals.

Prayer can also help us make the right decisions and stay on the right path. By asking for God's guidance, we can make choices that align with His will and purpose for our lives. This can help us avoid pitfalls and stay on track toward achieving our goals.

Moreover, prayer can help us stay connected to God and trust in His plan for our lives. When we pray, we acknowledge that we cannot accomplish our goals on our own and that we need God's help and support. This can help us cultivate a deeper sense of faith and trust in God's plan for our lives, even when things do not go as we expect or hope.

To make prayer a regular part of your life, set aside time each day to pray and seek God's guidance. This can include praying alone or with others, using prayer journals or devotionals, or simply talking to God throughout the day.

Incorporating biblical prayer into your life can help you gain insight and strength to help you achieve your goals. Whether it be for guidance, comfort, or strength, prayer can be a valuable tool in helping you focus on what is important and provide peace and clarity during difficult times. By trusting in God and seeking His will through prayer, you can find the courage to take risks and make changes necessary to reach your goals.

This is the confidence we have in approaching God: that if we ask anything according to his will, he hears us. - 1 John 5:14

Chapter 9

Christ Consciousness Meditation - Connect w/ your Christ like mind and accomplish all your goals.

Part 1: Knowledge

God -

Christ Consciousness is a timeless concept that involves connecting with our Christ-like mind and abilities to access a higher level of consciousness. The Bible makes several references to this idea, including the opening verse of the Gospel of John, which states, "In the beginning was the Word, and the Word was with God, and the Word was God" (John 1:1). This verse highlights the concept of Christ Consciousness during the creation of the world, suggesting that God utilized this power to bring about all the wonders of the world.

Throughout the Bible, we witness individuals tapping into their Christ-like mind and abilities to achieve great things. For instance, Moses parted the Red Sea and led the Israelites to freedom through God's guidance and his own faith. Similarly, Elijah performed miraculous feats such as calling down fire from heaven through his connection with God.

Jesus was the ultimate example of someone who could access this higher consciousness and abilities. He performed countless miracles, including healing the sick and bringing the dead back to life. His teachings and actions were rooted in love, compassion, and forgiveness, all of which are crucial components of Christ Consciousness.

Today, we can still tap into our own Christ-like mind and abilities through prayer, meditation, and other spiritual practices. Doing so allows us to access a higher level of consciousness and bring positive change into our lives and the world around us. Whether we seek guidance, healing, or simply a greater sense of peace, Christ Consciousness is a powerful tool that can help us achieve our goals and lead a more fulfilling life.

The Holy Spirit -

The idea of sudden, unexpected changes or transitions is a concept that can be found throughout the Bible. One example is the story of Saul or the Apostle Paul, who experienced a dramatic transformation on the road to Damascus. In an instant, he went from being a persecutor of Christians to a devoted follower of Christ. This sudden change was a result of the Holy Spirit working in his life.

Some may say that the Holy Spirit is Christ Consciousness or the Power of God itself. It is the divine energy and presence of God that fills us with spiritual power and helps us to live out our faith. One way that the Holy Spirit works in our lives is through the gifts that are given to believers.

The gifts of the Holy Spirit, also known as the spiritual gifts, are special abilities that are given to believers by the Holy Spirit. These gifts are described in the New Testament of the Bible, specifically in 1 Corinthians 12:4-11 and Romans 12:6-8. The gifts are:

Wisdom: The ability to understand and apply spiritual truths in practical ways.

Knowledge: The ability to understand the mysteries of God and the universe.

Faith: The ability to believe in God and His promises without doubt or fear.

Healing: The ability to bring physical or emotional healing to others through prayer or laying on of hands.

Miracles: The ability to perform supernatural acts that go beyond the laws of nature.

Prophecy: The ability to speak a message from God to others, usually involving foretelling or forth-telling.

Discernment: The ability to distinguish between truth and falsehood, good and evil.

Tongues: The ability to speak in a language that is not known to the speaker, often used in prayer and worship.

Interpretation of tongues: The ability to interpret the message of tongues for others.

These gifts are given to believers for the purpose of building up the church and spreading the gospel. It is important to note that not all believers receive the same gifts, and that no gift is more important than another. The gifts are to be used with humility, love, and discernment, for the glory of God and the benefit of others.

The Holy Spirit can work in powerful and unexpected ways, bringing about sudden changes or transitions in our lives. By embracing the gifts of the Holy Spirit, we can tap into this divine power and bring about positive change in the world around us. We must be open and receptive to the Spirit's leading, trusting that God has a plan and purpose for our lives.

People of the Old Testament -

Throughout the Old Testament, there are many stories of individuals who experienced divine intervention and were granted special abilities by God. These stories serve as examples of how the power of God can work in our lives and how we can access our own divine potential.

Jacob's ladder is a well-known story in which Jacob has a vision of a ladder connecting heaven and earth, with angels ascending and descending on it. This experience led to a transformation in Jacob's life and identity, and he became one of the patriarchs of the Jewish people.

Moses was granted the power to perform miracles, such as turning his staff into a snake and parting the Red Sea, which allowed the Israelites to escape from Egypt.

Joseph was able to interpret Pharaoh's dreams, which saved Egypt from famine. This is an example of how God can grant us insight and understanding to help others.

Samson was granted incredible physical strength by God, which he used to defeat the enemies of Israel.

David was known for his divine protection in battle and also had the gift of prophecy.

Elijah was a prophet who performed many miracles, including calling down fire from heaven and raising the dead.

Elisha was a disciple of Elijah and was granted many of the same powers as his mentor, including the ability to heal the sick and raise the dead.

Esther became queen of Persia and used her position to save the Jewish people from a plot to destroy them. This story shows how God can use our influence and power for good.

Solomon was known for his great wisdom, which was a gift from God. He was able to make wise judgments and decisions, and was also a skilled poet and writer. In addition, he was able to build the temple of God in Jerusalem, which was a great feat of engineering and architecture.

These stories illustrate how the power of God can work in our lives and how we can access our own divine potential. They show us that through faith, prayer, and spiritual practices, we too can access a higher level of consciousness and bring about positive change in the world around us.

Jesus -

Jesus is one of the most well-known and revered figures in history, recognized by many as the embodiment of Christ Consciousness. He is believed to have been the son of God, born of the Virgin Mary, and was sent to earth to redeem humanity from sin and reconcile them with God.

One of the central aspects of Jesus' ministry was his ability to perform incredible miracles, which are believed to have been an image of his connection to God. These miracles included healing the sick, feeding thousands with a few loaves and fishes, and even raising the dead.

Jesus' healings were not just physical, but also spiritual and emotional, as he was able to heal the whole person. This was a result of his connection to a higher power, which he referred to as his Father in heaven. Jesus' teachings emphasized love, compassion, forgiveness, and the importance of treating others with kindness and respect.

Jesus' ultimate sacrifice on the cross and subsequent resurrection is believed to have redeemed humanity from sin and reconciled them with God. His life and teachings continue to inspire millions of people around the world, and his example serves as a powerful reminder of the potential for all individuals to access the power of Christ Consciousness and make a positive impact on the world.

The Disciples -

The power of Christ Consciousness in the New Testament is not limited to Jesus alone, as his disciples were also able to access the power of God and perform incredible feats. One of the most notable disciples was Paul, who was granted the gift of speaking in tongues and the ability to perform miracles, including healing the sick and casting out demons.

Peter is another disciple who demonstrated the power of Christ Consciousness. When Jesus called him out of the boat to walk on water with him, Peter stepped out in faith and was able to walk on water for a short time. This story is a powerful example of the power of Christ Consciousness, as Peter was able to perform the seemingly impossible task of walking on water through his connection to Jesus.

The disciples of Jesus were chosen by him to spread his teachings and continue his work after his death and resurrection. While they did not possess supernatural powers like Jesus, they were empowered by the Holy Spirit to perform miracles and healings in his name. For example, they were able to heal the sick and disabled, speak in tongues to communicate with people from many different nations, cast out demons in Jesus' name, perform miracles such as feeding the 5,000 with just a few loaves and fish, and preach the gospel with boldness and courage even in the face of persecution and death.

Through their connection to Christ Consciousness, the disciples were able to tap into the power of God and perform incredible acts that went beyond the laws of nature. They were able to spread the message of Jesus' love and salvation to the world, and continue his work on earth long after his death. Their example teaches us that through our own connection to Christ Consciousness, we too can access the power of God and perform incredible feats that can change the world.

The Church -

The Bible mentions Christ Consciousness throughout, suggesting that God, The Holy Spirit, figures of the Old Testament, Jesus, and his Disciples were all able to access the power of God to create the world and perform miracles.

Similarly, the power of the Church comes from the Holy Spirit, which indwells and empowers believers. This power is evident in the way the Church has transformed countless lives throughout history, bringing hope to the hopeless, healing to the sick, and love to the brokenhearted.

The Church exercises its power primarily through evangelism. The Church has been given the mandate to spread the Gospel message to all nations, baptizing them in the name of the Father, Son, and Holy Spirit. Through this mission, the Church has brought countless souls to Christ, helping people find salvation and forgiveness for their sins.

In addition to evangelism, the Church is also called to heal the sick, cast out demons, and perform miracles. These gifts of the Holy Spirit are still present in the Church today, and many believers have experienced miraculous healings, deliverance from addictions, and other supernatural interventions.

The power of prayer is another significant aspect of the Church's power. Through prayer, believers can connect with God and intercede for others. The Church has seen the power of prayer bring about miraculous healings, changed hearts, and even societal transformation.

Finally, the Church has the power to bring about social change through acts of compassion, charity, and justice. The Church is called to care for the poor, the marginalized, and the oppressed, and to fight against injustice and inequality. By working together and using their collective resources, the Church can make a significant impact in the world, bringing about positive change and transformation.

It is important to note that these powers and abilities are given for the purpose of building up the church and spreading the gospel, not for personal gain or selfish ambition. As believers, it is important to seek God's will and ask for His guidance in all aspects of our lives. We may not all be granted miraculous powers or abilities, but we can still access the power of Christ Consciousness through prayer and meditation. By focusing on our relationship with God and seeking to do His will, we can accomplish great things and make a positive impact in the world around us.

In conclusion, the power of God is not limited to certain individuals in the Bible. Rather, it is available to all believers through the Holy Spirit. By exercising this power through evangelism, healing, prayer, and social action, the Church can impact lives, bring about transformation, and ultimately bring glory to God.

Part 2: Action

How to use your 8th Prosperity Tool

As we seek to deepen our understanding of the Bible and our faith, it's important to explore the concept of Christ Consciousness and how it can transform our lives. Christ Consciousness is a way of accessing a higher level of awareness and understanding, allowing us to create positive change in ourselves and in the world.

One of the key aspects of Christ Consciousness is connecting with our unique spiritual gifts, such as wisdom, discernment, and intuition. By embracing these gifts, we can gain insight into ourselves and the world around us, making decisions that align with our highest good.

Another essential aspect of Christ Consciousness is recognizing the interconnectedness of all things. We are all part of a greater whole, and by honoring these connections, we can cultivate greater empathy and compassion for others. This can lead to deeper relationships and a more harmonious world.

Practicing Christ Consciousness can also help us find greater purpose and meaning in our lives. By connecting with our spiritual gifts and recognizing our interconnectedness, we can gain a deeper understanding of our place in the world and the impact we can have. This can inspire us to live with greater intention and make choices that align with God's values and beliefs.

Ultimately, Christ Consciousness is a way of living that allows us to connect with God and access a higher level of awareness. By embracing this practice, we can tap into our unique gifts and abilities, recognize our interconnectedness with others, and live with greater purpose and meaning. As we continue to grow in our faith, let us strive to cultivate Christ Consciousness in our lives and in the world around us.

Jesus answered, "I am the way and the truth and the life. No one comes to the Father except through me. - John 14:6

Chapter 10

Holy Spirit Giving - Systematic giving from the heart

Part 1: Knowledge

Giving from the kindness of your heart is a beautiful act of generosity that can bring joy to both the giver and receiver. It is an expression of selflessness and humility, and can be a powerful way to demonstrate God's love to others. Whether it be a kind word, a helping hand, or a monetary donation, giving with a pure heart can have a profound impact on those around you.

In order to truly give from the kindness of our hearts, it is essential to recognize that all blessings come from God. We must give without expecting anything in return and remember to give all the glory to Him. By using our gifts and talents to serve others, we can show our gratitude for the blessings in our own lives and give back to those in need.

When we give from the kindness of our hearts, we demonstrate love and humility. It is a way to serve others and show God's love in action. It is also an opportunity to spread positivity and joy, bringing light to those who may be struggling. By giving in this way, we can be assured that all the glory goes to God and that our actions will bring hope and comfort to those around us.

It is important to approach giving with kindness and consideration, taking into account the needs and feelings of the recipient. Giving with empathy and respect demonstrates a sincere desire to help and can make a lasting impact. Whether it be through a simple compliment, a helping hand, or a donation, giving from the heart has the power to spread love and make the world a more loving and just place.

In conclusion, giving from the kindness of your heart is a beautiful and powerful act of love that can make a difference in the lives of others. By recognizing God's blessings in our own lives and using our gifts and talents to serve others, we can spread joy and hope to those around us. May we all strive to approach giving with humility, kindness, and consideration, bringing light and love to those in need.

Part 2: Action

How to use your 9th Prosperity Tool

Giving from the heart is a powerful tool that can help us achieve our goals in many ways. It can help us build meaningful relationships with others, give us a sense of purpose, and provide an opportunity to make a positive difference in the world.

When we give from the heart, we become more aware of the needs of others. This heightened awareness can help us stay focused on our own goals by reminding us of the bigger picture and what truly matters. By giving, we also cultivate a sense of purpose and fulfillment that comes from helping others.

Moreover, giving from the heart can help us develop a sense of gratitude and appreciation for the things we have. By recognizing the needs of others, we can gain a new perspective on our own blessings and feel grateful for what we have. This sense of gratitude can be a powerful tool in helping us stay motivated and focused on achieving our goals.

In addition to building gratitude, giving from the heart can help us build meaningful relationships with others. By giving, we can connect with people on a deeper level and build trust and rapport with them. This can lead to opportunities and collaborations that can help us achieve our goals and make a positive impact in the world.

To tap into the power of giving, start by finding ways to give back to others. This can be as simple as volunteering at a local charity or offering to help a friend in need. Look for opportunities to give from the heart and make a positive difference in the world.

In conclusion, giving from the heart is a powerful tool that can help us achieve our goals and make a positive impact in the world. By giving, we can build meaningful relationships with others, find purpose and fulfillment, and develop a sense of gratitude for what we have. So, make giving a regular part of your life and watch as it transforms your perspective and helps you achieve your goals.

Freely you have received; freely give. - Matthew 10:8

Chapter 11

Keep Studying - Never Stop Learning

Part 1: Knowledge

The pursuit of knowledge should never be underestimated. Knowledge is the foundation of power, and the more we acquire, the more powerful we become. It's essential to embrace a lifelong learning mindset to stay ahead of the curve and remain competitive in our constantly evolving world.

Having a thirst for knowledge can open many doors and opportunities for personal and professional growth. It can help us gain an advantage in our careers, as well as deepen our understanding of the world around us. Knowledge is key to unlocking the mysteries of the universe, and it enables us to become better problem-solvers, critical thinkers, and even discover new and exciting things.

Moreover, knowledge is the bedrock of innovation and creativity, which are critical for success. Without knowledge, we are limited in our ability to think outside the box and generate new ideas. By seeking knowledge, we become more well-rounded individuals and more attractive to potential employers.

In conclusion, never stopping to seek knowledge is essential for personal and professional development. It opens new doors of opportunity, fosters critical thinking and problem-solving, and fuels innovation and creativity. To remain competitive and successful in today's fast-paced world, we must cultivate a love of learning and embrace a lifelong pursuit of knowledge.

Part 2: Action

How to use your 10th Prosperity Tool

Continuous learning is a powerful tool of personal growth and development. In a constantly evolving world where new information and knowledge are being generated at an unprecedented rate, it is vital to keep learning throughout our lives to remain relevant and competitive.

Learning offers many benefits, including broadening our knowledge base, enhancing our problem-solving skills, and improving our mental and physical health. When we learn new things, we stimulate our brains, which can help prevent cognitive decline and even reduce the risk of certain diseases. Moreover, learning can help us to become more confident and self-assured, leading to better decision-making and stronger relationships with others.

Furthermore, learning opens up new possibilities for personal and professional growth. Whether it's taking a course, reading a book, or attending a seminar, learning can help us to develop new skills that can lead to career advancement and increased earning potential. It can also help us to discover new passions and interests, leading to a more fulfilling life.

If you want to take your learning to the next level, consider using the 10th Prosperity Tool, which is to "invest in yourself and your own education." This tool encourages individuals to prioritize their personal and professional development by dedicating time and resources to continuous learning.

In conclusion, continuous learning is a vital component of personal growth and development. It is essential to keep our minds active and engaged, expanding our knowledge and skills to keep up with the changing world. Through learning, we can become more confident, successful, and fulfilled individuals, leading to a more satisfying and prosperous life. By investing in ourselves and our education, we can unlock new opportunities and achieve even greater success.

Oh, the depth of the riches of the wisdom and knowledge of God! How unsearchable his judgments, and his paths beyond tracing out! - Romans 11:33

9 798869 011817